NORTH

A Frank O'Hara Award Book

NORTH BY TONY TOWLE

1970   Published for the Frank O'Hara Foundation at

Columbia University Press   NEW YORK & LONDON

Some of these poems first appeared in two collections: *Poems*, 1966, and *After Dinner We Take a Drive into the Night*, Tibor de Nagy, 1968; in the anthologies *Poems Now*, Kulchur Press, 1966, *The Young American Poets*, Follett, 1968, *The Poets of the New York School*, University of Pennsylvania Press, 1969, *An Anthology of New York Poets*, Random House, 1970; and in the periodicals *C, Art and Literature, Lines, Mother, Clothesline, Elephant, Spice, The Paris Review, The World, Angel Hair, Extensions, Adventures in Poetry, Juillard, The New York Times*, and *Best & Co.*

Copyright © *1970 by Tony Towle*
ISBN: 0-231-03471-7
Library of Congress Catalog Card Number: 70-125619
Printed in the United States of America

for Irma

The annual Frank O'Hara Award for Poetry, named for the American poet who was killed in 1966, was established by the Frank O'Hara Foundation to encourage the writing of experimental poetry and to aid in its publication. The award is meant to carry on in some measure Frank O'Hara's interest in helping new poets in their work. Eligible for it are poets who have not had a book of poetry published or accepted for publication by a commercial or university press. Further information about the award is available from the Frank O'Hara Foundation at Columbia University Press, which published, in 1968, Spring in This World of Poor Mutts, by Joseph Ceravolo, and, in 1969, Highway to the Sky, by Michael Brownstein.

Born in New York on June 13, 1939, Tony Towle grew up in the city and studied at the New School. His poetry has appeared in several recent anthologies and in many magazines, including Paris Review, Art and Literature, The World, C, Mother, and Adventures in Poetry. Two collections of his poetry have been privately printed: Poems, 1966, and After Dinner We Take a Drive into the Night, Tibor de Nagy, 1968. Mr. Towle received the Gotham Book Mart Avant Garde Poetry Award in 1963 and the Poets Foundation Award in 1964 and 1966. He lives in New York with his wife, Irma, and their three-year-old daughter, Rachel.

The design for the jacket of the clothbound edition and the cover of the paperbound edition of this book is by Jasper Johns.

CONTENTS

NORTH

Tempted successfully to talk in the morning   ô rage
ô déséspoir
ô délices   ô bergères
already from an afternoon
limp and limpid in the shoals of repose
of bemusing crowds and currents with which to subject myself
direct and imagining
toward yet a 21st refreshment of the Christian era.
I disappear in the reaches of what I think I am doing,
stretched on its mossy banks in diaphanous oblivion
away from the mountainous stellar structures
which confine the newest materials
tied in aluminum weights to the furious morning brain;
as bellowing anarchy beats its skull
on the quaking cement of the city,
roots and herbs wait beneath for a crack, personae
watch from the fire escape and look once more at the sky,
subjected to the peculiarities of their drowsy creator
who has fled from the previous day
as a man waves to a train from a train,
protected from the exertion of stopping;

I arrive with the years of my sleep
past the age of Keats's conclusion,
radiant with nervousness and Hyperion's weight
"refusing forever the wishfulness of the visual,"
and suddenly consumed by a great sadness

as if autobiographical moments were being wasted,
and the blood pumped into the anguished perceptions
brings a thought of the night and the closing door. There is,
as I remember, a resistance to the silence of the bed,
to the lilacs and privet
which will presently bloom at the corners of the wool,
suspending the animal activity left in the room
and released to an interesting and serious province
with a random similarity to the sublime.
Planes go by in the dark.
Figures emerge from the closet
and I withdraw to allusion or awake in horror
to skim the oxygen from the air,
an element of which I am composed
and is common to everyone, like a suitcase.
I would try in vain to ignore the successes of the sight,
I who know so many excellent painters,
except that alone with my work the door is a blinding crack
and for seconds I am close to a rich and starless destination.

The daily search for the lyric concludes the night,
and painterly haystacks dot the distant imperial blue of awakening,
or one can remember that life can be terrible,
shaving with incompetence in the diminutive maturity of morning.
But I am alive and awake and see things clearly with a glance.
There is no door because it is not in the picture
but there are numerous windows in the clouds of life
and there is the liquid of my contemplating brain;
it thanks you for my contemporary adventure
when I look off with inspiration and forget who I am;
our incongruities are passed on to children,
a line of sorrowful trees awaits them in their books

but the voiceless sublime will accept my invitation at last

its excess, its assistance
which the milling public
nor you nor any discovering person
has seen but reeling with desire.

The two knights suggest to the king that he take the hero
into his confidence. The pantomimes are spaced to accommodate them.
It is a work of great beauty. It is night. Four boys
remain on the scene. They choose four girls. This is what happens:

Her beauty and her brains work like fire. She is shocked.
by his remark that he cannot spend too much time. We see grace of
body and mind being torn to pieces. Now begins the bitter aftermath:

Now the prayers of Orpheus are answered. It is the ancient myth of
Orpheus. Orpheus cannot console himself with his own song. The song
of the lyre is inadequate to his bereavement. Now he finishes the
song. Everything is green. Everything is splashed with color.

What I think in February is there for April.
In the mirror my guileless face, as opposed to my stomach
which has done abstraction a disservice.
Pinch yourself and look up at the spreading sky.
From it comes the barge of morning,
floating to where we are drifting to wake us up.
Behind it comes the barge of evening.
A strand of protoplasm hangs down from a tree.
An inquisitive frog approaches. From the dark
a pair of glowing eyes peer at you.
It is only a watching raccoon, or an owl.

We deal with the evil forces one by one,
the protoplasm, the slime, the different beasts
springing to life and desire.
The bed throws a blanket over the atmosphere.
It is not safe to step in the water with the fish.
It is not safe to walk in the sand or through the trees.

FOR JAMES COCO

The Bronx! The teeming Concourse, its viable
tradition of sex and stability,
where maidens pick at their food.
The winged horses of empire soar above Wall Street
and in the full flower of spring
miniature grapes are picked near City Hall.
Cards are dealt, money passes; peasants
carry groceries to the larders of the rich; candidates
for mayor weep at their plight and weep again
as each passes away, as we all must, to the great beyond.

But new constituents are born and votes are cast. On
some frosty morning the year comes to a close,
followed by bright January meals: a steaming lasagna,
at Jimmy's, devoured beneath an opulent tapestry,
richly embroidered with superb performances and enviable awards
which rise on the climbing fabric
to the attendant clusters of stars above
gleaming from the ceiling's midnight azure,
the approbation of merciless directors;
the audience is woven on the wall below, in velvet,
gowns and feathers, ermine and flowing silk,
a dazzling melange of evening urban charm.

Soon comes the Fourth of July, a festival day, but it is warm
and New Yorkers get nasty. They roam the streets
and sneer at your clothes. In the throes of humid frustration
they fumble with the lock on your door,
climb irritably through your windows,
or tighten their grip on your handbag,
murmuring some peculiar insights.
So people leave for the country and romp in the grass; donkeys
laden with faggots wend their campy way to Riis Park; girls
of our myriad shapes and nationalities
step out in the summer of perfect virtue, burst into bloom,
and are plucked, to maintain our city's ascendancy.

Through it all my poor delightful self-serving verse,
more archaic by the minute,
runs down the lanes in sparkling rivulets,
basking in the dreams of personality, in Poulenc's
exquisite self consciousness, in Satie's wit,
over the slips and into the bay, immersed in the glories of irony,
Neptune and his towering arm of water.

When a mayor dies, our bustle is confined momentarily:
the shoes of workers scuffling on the pavement,
actors rocketing to stardom,
the churning wheels of industrial development,
come sorrowfully to a halt and pay their respects.

My unconscious mind spun in delirium. The wings
are right over me and in a moment, the claws
will be ripping me apart. The pictures crowded in;
a tremendous blast of air swept over me,
at least that is what I told myself.

There is a great leap in thought. The scene
takes on a more brooding quality: I realize
that you are an enemy, a giant sphere
supported by the heavens. When you disappear
I return to my other identity.

The daffodils spring up, a fantasy of her own.
Not one skirt escaped her scissors. I knew
I had seen the last of her as she vanished into the sky.

The muse at daybreak stuttering, informs my bed,
pines in the scented winter air for poems,
and mumbles about the government and whether I should vote:

"The government stinks; withhold your vote of red and white
its hidden sea and blue of politic sky
which clouds the world and so to surround our realm."

Government would speak as well, from the vales of Abstraction,
who on the death of Pound will ramble on once more,
their inbred grandeur making you feel like a schmuck.
Milton of course could order these people around, God, Satan,
Liberty, Progress and the rest. To me God might say
You employ a distinctive style and I know who you are,
but you are not illuminating for me,
you do not give me any ideas, about myself, or what I have done.

Satan: Since you deal only with your own activity
and with immeasurable vanity,

I will eventually bring you something you dislike,
and in phrase of unshakable metaphor
as with that you think to spin out your life.

Satan concludes: You will have more poems than you hope
but more than you wish; your finger pressed to a difficult line,
your tongue on occasion piercing a word's transparency,
but my older tongue of iron comes inexorably to cover yours
and in your future is of greater eloquence.

The day half gone the muse and its servants fled,
a sandwich gone through you in enormity to Philadelphia,
cheese and milk flowing through you and into Boston,
air on its way to Minneapolis.

What a summer I had! diving and snuffling
in the brine needing a shave,
deep in the bristles which cut the sand,
or how baleful the option of going downstairs,
gum in colorful spots on the coat,
hearing the slosh of ambiguity.

So an evening alone is your chief stupidity,
the newspaper fumbling at your sleeve,
ingenuity burning through to your pants,
but happily the steam rising from you in pity
allows you a drift of the truly eternal,
the shuddering gauze of its door, your ass
resting and green on the floating resentful foliage.

What amusing solids. Several explain the world,
and presuming work to be liquid cool your faces
after the black and burning summer,
a salad for your paradise of disgust
which you have felt throughout the life
of the wind which spits at your work,
its fresh attack of spitting in idle moments.

If you walk slowly, out of breath, and think,
and breathe the air, on a coast,
arriving at the coast out of breath
and helpless, distressed about your conclusions
because it is evening and difficult to see,
then everything you sense may be enchanted, in a fugitive way,
as soon it will be a different situation.

1

A surgeon, his daughter, a chemist and some gentlemen.
The smile, of the daughter, warms the dead snow.
They are in the basement. They are on the roof,
a function of the shadowy street;
                              But you, divine perceiving light,
holding one's foot as we soak the rays of the sun
over an icy ocean of winter at sea, bring us our voices
as they would be in the movies, hoarse from the dialogue,
our dripping hands full of tobacco, our frozen eyes
watching the camera, our sensuality
folklore already captured by a review
in a comparison with the vivid past,
our development racing the comparison, an impression
racing the drug.

You, comprehensible light, may find us leaving,
presenting us as you wish. We understand the problems,
the highlights and shadows;
    . . . but the drug takes effect and we are doctors,

fumbling to open our eyes and hands; we think
the scalpel is something else. We say goodbye,
yelping and banging the door.
Circumstances fall into place and the pulse slows to normal.
He examines a liver and eats it. The shape of the liver
is repeated until he is depressed, the light revealing nothing else.

2

You open your eyes, the gentlemen disperse,
each to a situation
you will investigate when you are rested,
with mixed feelings and time for contemplation,
and things falling, in slow motion from the window, into place,
as falling from the highest place imagined
in the coming moment, has produced the effect of falling now,
and shows what is an orange falling from its place,
with later others, in disorder, also falling,
and the orange has fallen, into the water,
and we are free to see it disappear,
and unencumbered we go to the nearest place that is comfortable.

3

The idea stops, halts, abruptly.
A friend may enter the room, happy and alive,
talking and you listen but you are not sure.
You stand and listen.
We will feel better with each word tomorrow,
understanding the conversation differently and admiringly,
the words growing dense and great. When their greatness diffuses

we notice the colors of paint. Their delicate use astounds us,
the silver light at the top remains that color
as we wade, intoxicated with the warmth of the water,
the group of figures at the front, the bottom, conveying
the infinite satisfaction their presence makes possible,
delighting us with the colorless air they breathe,
stirring the breathtaking length of our trip like a fluid.

In the morning we are set in rows and given problems. Who
finishes quickly is given one more, more complicated,
until finally things are perfected and we disperse, as
gentlemen, having started with nothing and excelled in everything,
our projects and accomplishments nearby in the light,
illuminating our successive details.
There is a thought. The light is excluded from the trees
and the group of people are fools, departing, leaving
a woman, naked and pensive, near a cloud, and
watching it from the distant side of a space
covered with inches of water. She turns her head,
thinking, as I write, crossing her mind.

An Arcadian breeze from the southwest
holds the shimmering spoon of today
in 80 degrees, and it is certain
even in water, the ocean of summer,
that like your predecessors and with their civilized grief
that you live in the sky, among fish,
Romantic graphics, and the earliest airplanes,
that there is no ventilation in our wool of 1870 July,
that barrels horses and sweat appear along lower Broadway
to expire in the streets with 19th century expansion;
where else can one conceive stupendous odes but in the sky
and take responsibility for the sea, the sky,
and our distribution among the species;
where else do you hear with composure
the screams of memorable adventures
from far below in the century's night
whose beauty you evade to capture;
a condition understood when you first spoke,
in post-Depression Manhattan, taken to the suburbs
to continue speaking, with a sense of the Dionysian air
refining your words at this later date
when it is a great odyssey to read and write,
to be flattered by the enjambments of contracts Ron
and David's anthology and Paul Carroll's and as it is water
here in the sky it is also the grass, eternal blanket,
that you face staring up, incredible glance, or looking beneath.

The great worm of the north, in whose footsteps we tread,
eludes us with a thousand lightnings.
However the bus, the nourishment of the city, pulls in,
and nothing has been accomplished though beauty
interrupts constantly, interpolating a row of moments
like a pink balustrade basking in the sun.

The buses and planes go forward in clouds of yeast and salt,
lurching over the pipes and turbines of the city
as Wyoming would slide down the coast of Norway
and I look from the plane as from the vantage point of a roof
to see the Lefrak Building shielding my eyes from Manhattan.
Lefrak, whose first name has escaped me—like Catherine
the Great's last—into the wild blue,
but who with Moses, whose first name is an anticlimax,
has left us the Queens of today and tomorrow.

We surprise the great worm in the frozen waste of his sleep.
Our magic ax and feather do their work
and the monster lies helpless in scattered and giggling pieces.
The five boroughs are safe and rainbows arch over the brick,
bright birds with their pinions are free to range once more,
but in whose colorful wake our hurtling plane seems spiritless,
planning to touch only Chicago and perhaps Detroit,
with a landing in the meantime however subtle meaning an emergency,
with no one congenial until reaching the ground, parachutes billowing,
and relaxing on the train back to New York, the parachute as a souvenir.

The last idiot elegy, a beer
dries over my hand as if I breathe
an evaporation not a woman
with its implications of a sough
going up to poetic clouds
in a billowing smoke of triumph,
the speeding Nebraska plains
of a hill distant and opportune
in the throat, a typical thing
to choke on.

To grow with the restive prices
and talk through the march of real estate,
the adhesive blue of the eye
which raises the spinning earth
and the beauty coming easily from you
before your eyes to balance your stare
is only the subway on the last day
before the year begins to stir
to lift you awake and scheming
into its limits.

And you return
where the celebrated deepening of your wish
yearns for desire in luxury
in the composition of sitting down,
the transparent allegory of tears,
for the insufferable humanity of art.

We are watching for someplace to eat. We feel we are prey
for the insane scavengers of the air. We cannot make up our minds
and race five hundred miles away from our hosts.

I begin to feel passion.
I walk back and forth and it is a slow movie,
without the interest of acting, only walking.
Far from my prying eyes she strips off her clothes.
Oh for the wings of a bird.

The record slows down;
sweat falls on the instruments;
the musicians are bored.
A hand comes from the clouds to give me a poem.
I accept it and we shake hands.

The incident with the hand haunted me for the rest of my life.
I began to gasp. It is time to sing the death song,
clearing the tops of the trees, hearing the glass
from the window and the traffic from the street.
Each year is a supermarket, no each year is captured by a word,
repeated with nostalgia, overwhelmed by ineptitude,
dropping to the ground and rolling down the bowling alley of the sky.

A skylight of wire and glass with a retractable roof
holds the pan of boiling thoughts,
bubbles of air freezing and thawing
come upward from the hardened concrete,
and lends a feeling of drama and steel framework.

We think we are housed in a golden dome,
with carved and trailing flowers, with nymphs
to draw close from the brilliant heavens,
in stacks of glittering elements,
our attachment to the people we know and space.

We move along in the space, its innumerable
walks along the beach but really New York,
summer, fall, blazing away
and nothing further from the truth.

We eat and hear as your kiss descends
over the piano and the sky.
The tide rushes out of a box and I am dead.
Prokovieff is dead as I am.
On the day of judgment, when we are released,
we will hear the rain and the thunder
and miles of cars will stop in their tracks.
The line down the highway is white,
the color of the sky before Prokovieff.
At the beginning I am here behind the typewriter.
I wander off to the cliffs to see the sharks
looking for a finger or bloody popcorn or a ruined doll.
I throw them a ruined doll.
The camera moves in for a close-up. I adjust my tie
but it focuses on my cigarettes, Pall Mall Filters,
and the shining gold pack which contains them.
The camera goes on across the crowd.
We have five seconds on camera, a daguerrotype,
the room is upside down and objects fall with a crash.
Then a picture of an airplane.
The airplane or the sun is upside down.
It is the sun, which falls like an egg onto a plateau.
The real sun burns it to a disgusting omelette.
The sun also drains the color from the words, the moon
turns them to chalk and they collapse.

An engineer pushes a button in the mountains,
and another mountain lifts itself
and slides into the lake,
revealing a patchwork of interesting minerals.
The air follows us as we walk along.

Look at all this junk. My glass is cracked suddenly.
Look at the punch leaking out onto my sleeve.
That is the way I see things,
that or locked up in storage bins, alongside one another,
and hanging from my tie as from a dangling rope,
ending up in the same intrigue of thoughts,
becoming a digestible poison,
and the nerve-ends evolved to cope with instant danger
do not know what to tell the brain so they think about it.

Back in the mountains. The engineer pulls a switch,
and a mountain,
making a quiet sliding sound, lifts itself
and slides into the lake.
There is bound to be a breeze now,
we are a hundred feet in the air.
There is no shock, just a quick vibrant lift.
The air comes with us,
a warm halo of fog and icy water with no sense of motion.

Down, on the great avenue of the nation, finds Florida,
a rented car and dopey blonde to set the mood in a few seconds;
or summer, on the streets of San Francisco's walking journalism.
But I'm really thinking about the end of the year
and relentless poets practising the art of boredom,
new poets of England and America expanding the syrup of dullness,
their voluminous republic and constitutional monarchy, the Dunciad.
Today Pope would be working on nothing else,
forsaking England to cope with America,
its swarms of universities each with its major poet,
the batteries of Pulitzers filling the sky with fumes,
as National Book Awards settle on the weary hand
and ingeniously awarded prizes from the Mid-West
confound the senses with their vapors.
In Chicago *Poetry* ensnares a readable poem,
to strangle it in fifty sluggish pages.
In New York our *Review of Books* goes on with its monologue,
leading the heaviest prose from its ancient purple
into a slumbering gray. Or the *Partisan Review* stumbles forward,
from the smoke of its burning Moral Issues,
to seize the last of the air the moment Con Edison sleeps;
and from the gloom of midnight the heroic Evergreen emerges,

trailing the sewage of Literary Emancipation,
decked with the charms of Circulation and Advertising
to ward off the spirits of originality,
and proves each month the hypothesis
that writing and shit are one.
But I'm also thinking about Democracy,
where our humble president* postpones the debut of a princess†
to tell us the state of the union may be a cliché after all,
as the princess stands in for an actress
to remind us that elegance after all may be truly empty.
They are taking the breath from the start of the year
which should open its mouth to an Augustan Age,
blowing away those whom Eliot has crushed but who remain,
those who are sat on by Pound or by Williams,
who open Ginsberg or Ashbery and come away cursed,
but from January comes the barbarous breath of a winter still with us,
the polluted streams of England and now France,
the arid wind west of New Jersey,
the legislative nerves of Washington quickened
to the possibilities of artistic government, poets becoming politicians,
judges becoming critics, critics as dreary as ever.
It seems that your back hurts. Yes well that's possible.

* Johnson   † Radziwill

Look into this suitcase,
what do you see?
A black raincoat.
Look again.
A blue raincoat.
Again.
A black raincoat.
Get on this plane;
what's the problem?
I don't think it's safe.
It's safe, just get on.

The steel blades, or wood, whirl to exhaustion
but the vehicle doesn't move. I light up a cigarette,
nervously at first, but becoming more calm
as the flame grows larger and destroys the tobacco,
and the smoke overcomes the landscape
which enables the plane to get up in the air.

Now what's the problem?
The cigarette's gone out.
Where are you by this time?
Over New Zealand I think.
Have you ever been to New Zealand?
I was born there, near Wellington.
That's interesting; what now?
I'd like something to eat.

The lakes and the trees are very beautiful in New Zealand.
I have sat down near a small lake and I am going to look at it.

The dawn of opening the book: Page one, I close the eyes of the person.
Above the eyes are the imaginable fears, decayed and coming forward.
He is safe within the eyes, red and closed, the exploding color
which fills the mirror.

From the water we take to the air. I open my eyes, wet and breathing,
and by a miracle grateful for the haze, the breeze, the endless mist.
A glass is raised to see the landscape better. Most of it is gone.
There is a classic cloud, drifting with the brush to the end of the color,
the blue of what is seen languidly and created.

Page two, with shouting and blood as the roof of bricks gives way.
A survivor receives a farm and dies, happy or sad
to hear the windows being closed, the air smothered,
with no oxygen and nothing will burn.

You learn new things every week.
You go nowhere in the way that you expect.
Awash on the streets you save money on linens and shirts.
You count and examine your change.
Something hideous falls on you, as from a great height.
For if you insist on writing there will be these shapes
throughout an evening,
beginning with poetry and ending on a slope of prose.

Sure I don't have anything to do with the moon
because boring people will land there,
nothing to do with the century
except to swallow its apple of sophistication
difficult but no wider than a stopping train,
running by the houses and killing the grass
here on Long Island where you walk around
and have not seen the moon for so long
in the haphazard temerity of keeping awake.

But even so, on an infinite train of thought
you look to your syntax for an exquisite mist,
the flowers of Park Avenue Madison Avenue
which like your suit are covered with a thin film.

Poem

FOR JIM ROSENQUIST

The car stops like a mortar shell exploding in history.
Powerful forces are at work, pulling at us,
from the kitchen, where it is time to eat,
from the roof, where the gray-green waves . . .

From the hill ideas fall into the sea.
A stream of water jets up from the gravel and the sea,
where we think we are living, skimming over the water,
to polar regions and refreshing ice.

The powerful forces have stopped dead.
I tie my tie and don't talk.
Soon the tie is in shreds and I am off,
up the wall ahead of the leaves,
leaving a trail of dust and soot.

Across the yard are safety and morsels of food.
High up are the great mirror and comb,
poignant and full of fun.
From Lakeville we drive to the station,
slowing down at a steak house,
the electric fan blowing its breeze.

The gulls glide, in 1939, into the bonus of another country,
the balloons and machinery of all the Europes and Americas,
a hundred million words at ease in the river,
rising as I think about myself,
and in the history of my ears making a beginning of the frontier.

Ah the complete bunker of the earth and its dirt flying up,
across our view at the peak of the centuries,
pauses and silence as subtle as the wine of Bordeaux, and as words
coming time after time before the vigilance of your dizzying indulgence.

An incredible weight hangs today from my evasions,
you, and my biography which gets a little endless,
your immortal heart disappearing endlessly in the crisis,
slowly to be clear, and quickly to be interesting,
as we stay in the tonic of the bad air.

So what is the distinction of the river drawing you forward,
away from the restiveness of a vast American poetry
which you created with an unfathomable love.
You will be with the few of the past great enough to talk to,
as the remainder of this century of poetry begins to suffer
and your work will burst repeatedly our silence of unbearable memory.

August and then December will close the century
O air of your dreams descending on my day off.

Now it is April, then the great bull of May,
and then it will be my birthday and time for presents and the beach.
That's when the poetry of summer descends on you
if you are a poet, and the metaphors emit an enormous heat,
tapering off to the luxuriant melancholy verse of fall.
Then 1968 and my vote for president, and January 1969 and 70. By
this time my poetry improves, a compliment to the new administration.
I suppose that other people's poetry will also have improved,
worse luck, and there will be new painters and paintings,
and a host of movies which I won't keep track of,
or as Johnson said of Pope, considering the English climate
what would an Englishman want with a grotto.
As an American I should enjoy a grotto.
The walls would be fragrant with the spirits of the earth
and in general be like a symphony by Shostakovitch,
very entertaining, a vodka and tonic made with Russian vodka.
The clocks' stopping means I'm waiting for you to get home;
dinner and the television of Sherlock Holmes and Watson
shaping our evening with Hollywood precision;
beautiful cinematography and the pork chops this April
since they're yours and with the curtains drawn
spring in the area is a more delightful place in which to be.

"We Water Islanders are very proud of our heritage, our clams,
and our sand. Teddy Roosevelt used to come here,
and the salt air, our link with the past, revives us.
More and more we speak French on Water Island.
Since the German invasion we nestle in our rugged coves
and fuse our diverse citizenry."

The wings of the horizon glide into the foreground
and at any moment the results may become gruesome.
Razor-edged metal can take off an arm or a leg; sand,
rough as a rasp, can take out a piece of flesh the
size of an orange, and stones may cut like knives. The
ocean can follow, rising like a black demon, to swallow everything.

In general Fire Island is valuable, the scorching air and
the eeriness, the avalanche of sand, the seventeen

cubic miles of deck, the succession of people to amuse
until they stop from a sense of order, cushioned by turbulent gas,
cleaving a wake of digression to flee the chaotic,

and Frank's Love Poems (Tentative Title) are on Fire Island,
creating a view from Davis Park to the Pines
and they clarify the sky and the sea so the eye may pass between
when you paid five dollars instead of two
not arriving at 57th Street in his lifetime of art;

Well it's worth a lot more than five dollars
I know it is
and there are no more references on Water Island; No. 2
White Street, No. 2 Front Street, No. 3 North Moore Street,
240 West Broadway, 94 Greenwich Street, 227 West Broadway,
25 Charlton Street, 181 Front Street, all, marine breeze,
as they take in the sun and you imagine each, a function of the
1830's, the bay, the silence of Patchogue, the great North Atlantic

We manipulate like archeologists
from above their creation our picturesque conceits,
the urine twisting and turning for a few seconds,
to end in a high-velocity spray
onto the historical efforts of civilizations
and the imagined life styles of their individuals
redolent in the steam of geographical light.
A slightly far-fetched metaphor one might say? A futile
trip down the sides of inverted cones and triangles
until the monstrous verbosity gives itself up, rising
in the quest of evaporation to the top of the bay overhead? Hardly
do I finish when the decrepit creatures of hard-hitting realism
come wailing to the edge of my lunatic breakers
which collapse in confusion in that righteous but searing gaze.

The colorful bay, with its mystifying reality,
stretches beyond the colorful motorboats racing,
and the wonderful August clouds.
Unfolded chairs for the vacationing idle
in the blue of spotless shade with icy refreshments.
Take a glass, a set of beads
and a bookcase. Break them with a hammer,
and ship their remains to a literate citizen of Jakarta.

His skin is made up of layers, the first
resisting the package and its treasures, but in the second,
a tiny world, he steps back,
as carpenters work on his house
with the quiet saw of the Indonesian sky.

Corn   mollusks   smoking edible shellfish
Swallows go by and more shellfish crawl by,
in the water and ideas of fate   Boaters
get up with their wives and go forward,
monuments to the continent and quivering life.

The shellfish rest in the dark of a pure tranquility
and dinner is held pensively in the throat;
the sun far away in its struggle
from the divisive twinges of multiple anticipations,
the angels who cryptically flap their wings
and leave the night to my calm disinterest
for a break in the clouds of pure tranquility,
the wives of the yachtsmen getting up, piercing the air
as living arrows, the plateaux of their ambitious vacations,
raining the dark with suffering moisture.

1

The terrifying question was this:
What was dream and what was reality?
Thus day had followed night and night had followed day.
On weekends I listened to the call of the sea.
The rest of the week I carried on my research.

2

It is impossible to frighten a woman who is in love with you.
The crackle of flames and pungent smoke poured from the house,
our lips uniting in a kiss that tasted of blood.
Then I would wake up.
This time the dream was intense, quick, and brutally concise.

3

An idea obsessed me and I needed the shades of night.
Her sons are dead and her husband shot himself.
I could imagine them doing that and my veins
jumped with excitement: the incessant and threshing
roar of vegetation such as the wildest gale had never produced.

We put our heads here, and see nothing but beautiful yellow flowers.
We notice them because they are a different color,
having just come from a green so extraordinary
that we would have been there forever.
Previously we discovered the intensity of red,
asea with carnations and tulips. It is no matter
that you are oblivious, you are already there,
fitting into a number of years;
the sun revolves in its glory,
the animals bite the grass;
and when they are fat we will bite them,
chasing them over the hills to work up our appetites.
The bluejay flies overhead, the frog keeps pace with you on the ground;
the antelope runs before and the lion behind.
It is Friday on the gilded path to the bank with these creatures,
the clear magnificent river and paper one fords to cash one's check,
the lettuce you buy for the rabbits, or the birds
beating their wings to a standstill over the rooftops
in the effort poem after poem to be somewhere else
and to say nothing about it in the attempt to support yourself;
to scatter your sense among the planets
which you notice are all the same color
like the dishes washing themselves in the kitchen
which you notice because you are in the same room
which is variable as you drink forever.

FOR IRVING AND LUCY SANDLER

"My career has been spent as a courtier,
and a familiar of the court and the king.
I am Velasquez.
It is difficult to explain myself;
Caravaggio is a buffoon,
my six year old son could do better."

"Ah, yes, Velasquez. When I am admiring his work
I feel this twinge of impatience;
there are so many improvements to make
I do not know where to begin.
I am Manet. Everything is
hopeless in this miserable century."

"When Manet comes floating up
to our great studio in the sky,
I will give him a sound thrashing,
signed, Rubens, 1862."

I am ill, indisposed, dizzy. I have a cough. Where were you born?
Are you alone? How many are you? Have you lost too much blood? Let
me see your tongue. The skin is broken out. I don't like this room.
Let me examine your eye. You cannot move your elbow or your knee.
I have no money. Perhaps they will lend you some money. I want a priest.
Do you want a priest? Give me a package of cigarettes. We have
no cigarettes. Anything else? Nothing else.

The bone is broken and the area is swollen. You need aspirin and iodine,
a bandage and boric acid. I have lost my glasses. I have broken my glasses.
You need rest and quiet. Do you feel cold? There is someone to see you.
I am expecting someone. The sun and the moon are out. The stars are out.
Go four blocks and turn left.

In the rain what is there to do, what to play.
I ride beginning to doze, underground to the Bronx,
on a horse, under Manhattan like undigested pork,
unfortunate fish bouncing dead off the walls.
From the Bronx we drive, to Labrador, in Canada,
at the end of September, the sea full of hidden rocks.
Near the top of a mountain come up from the sea
we begin to see the danger of our experiment.
A little powder and the mountain is gone,
and clinging to an oar we are in the black water.

A voice rings out, the stranger chuckles,
and our reverie flees like a running dog.
Men and women come forward to shake our hands.
Bystanders take us to the café. In the café
the sun comes at midnight, burns our faces with liquor
and comes up in the morning. In the morning air we divide,
extending our thoughts and going on like birds,
over the sleeping thieves and invisible grass for them.
A breath of cold air and the flight is ending,
covering the grass and the rocks with her hair,
speeding the turn of the seasons and their grief,
our red mouths visible and the white sky full of clouds.

Second Pythian

FOR RON PADGETT

Lawyers inform their clients?   It is possible to guess

O matchless reclining marble flower of my dream

Do bears shit in the woods?   A hooded figure

scurries off

        into the years

holding his nose   of gray dawn

        (cough)

        in conversation

under the light of earth

        as researchers

    starting to smell and

        at work

        like the flight of a baseball

    on its voyage of truth

        I'm serious

    but alas

my crippling incurable disease

        which tires my muse

and confines my weary body

        mumbling

                                        to this accursèd chair

as my peers disport   hitting and fielding
grounders and line drives   the gentle sky
the cheerful robin redbreast   quiet lawns
of curious onlookers   pushing
in at the sides

               to wrap it up

                                  with zany scholarship

      decibels

                        in the foam of Western sport

                           Glowing June sunshine

I wish it the best possible success

The fire goes over the same place
and what does it relate to.
The sky is unpainted. The unpainted walls
turn out to be endless, and have wall sockets
into which are plugged appliances;
the wheels turn, the lights flash, steel balls
roll from one side of a box to another. I pull
the curtain across it and turn to its neighbor:
a lever releases colors, containing words,
which float through my eyes
causing sleeplessness so that I continue.

There is an effect of water.
The reefs and the rocks cut the water into
sheets of light, linked to the spectators:

two figures who are later gathered into a group
for the expression of a theme:

oblique lines, ascending from right to left
toward a mysterious forest hazy with light:

blue; the effort succumbs to academicism and
the movement comes to an end

Today the phantoms pass through rock.
The phantoms move higher in the rock, the smoke,

the fumes, and the powdered ash.
Instinctively I scale a tree, I vanish.
The clouds are torn apart to show the moon;
he drops to a bench; the telephone rings,
a hypnotic background for the words.

The green figures move forward and the objects grow larger,
explorers of the sky, exploring the earth immersed in water,
1967 with its fatal look of artificial brevity,
your life as if an illusion putting you near the window,
and promptly all the winds and currents ruffle the curtains.

The humid surroundings, a transparent lizard
under the leaves and stretching its rubber-like plastic
across the room, protruding with our European selves,
show that we valiantly dig at the earth, poise
on the brink of adventure, or blister the flatulent sky.
In other words you are held, amused, peacefully in the grass
o beautiful art springing to mind, as we are the supreme judges.

Or perhaps you have forgotten an important exaggerated phrase,
and your words spread over the stones in a pure grove of the specific,
and you speak only the names of the bellowing animals, plants and trees
which blind you touch; ships, insects peopling the forests, etcetera.
The labyrinth speaks from its precipice, its outline shoots in a curve
through the chemical air, in addition to writing the script.

O miracles of divine reaches and words spinning from infancy
and whose business and indispensible references are not known,
your story is truly a story to treasure, distilled intoxicant that it is,
saying that I am a synonym for the relaxed and drifting universe,
a mere summary holding my attention over the thundering firmament.

I am shouting tonight from the frost
and ruin of war,
to everyone in the bitten world
I have ever seen!
I am known to you desiccated swine
only in translation.
I stalk raging from this place!

Flowers grow in the narrow charming streets.
Talented people draw them,
and greatness is born! An imbecile
thinks of a breast, writes,
and withers to dust in the pale moonlight.
Phase IV, Biology, pulling at the petals,
lighting Winstons, pot and wood,
a package of Kents, gray wood,
gray ice, a nice yellow scarf.

The friendly Stock Exchange, debentures,
a nice lunch, ravens and talk of the afterlife. If we rise
gasping, again from the dead, and wish to hunt,
we seek the lumbering bear, the fox
or the bounding leopard, assuming their trials
and their empty balloons of speech,
as cars go by at the end of day
holding the men of the cities
and filling his creeping roads with travel.
I join them in its perilous toast
and follow them down the roads.

But a ghost may alight on the feathery swiftness of a raven
to flee the gloomy grave. Through the fences at night
rabbits hurry by, holding our shadowy souls with ease;
the badger returns for more;
he rises aloft, in patterns, lines and dots;
we give up our lives in his singular forest,
departing from North America.

Poets, Inc

FOR KENWARD ELMSLIE

The owl that I am leaves in a whoosh of classical euphuism
for a nap in the grass of the morning sun
and forgets that poems have to be exciting
and that two days ago I didn't know what euphuism meant
and now I know in the morning sun
that my life has been a succulent euphuism.

By afternoon impressions are riding the crest,
compassionate of small town life;
kitchen fixtures and colorless posters
descend through the air of clichés done to a turn.
I tend to write of things descending in the air,
but nothing relieves its microbiology.
I think of Apollinaire, but what happens
from Maine to Sacramento is politicians,
and nothing from Wantagh to Bellmore but travel itself.

If I could stop and relate this all to prosody
or a cohesive method, they would let go of me.
If some intriguing yet traditional versification
arrived, I could be on my way,
suffused with the crimson light of the brain's hot blood,
but now I must sleep, some day I will write again.

There is a forest where you are overjoyed,
absent with vapors,
and in whose teeth you dismount,
amiable in delight.

So that you can meet the love of your life
who wears the most shining dress obtainable,
whose footfall is the red tide and swimming gulf
you have remembered.

She feels in her legs a crimson flower
attracting the tongues of fantasy
which prowl upwards with appetite
to the exciting gate.

Each year our group holds a ceremony
at the grave of some great poet, singing
and paying tribute to his memory
for some great poems he has left to be read and remembered.
Last spring, Edwin Denby, Kenneth Koch, John Ashbery,
Jimmy Schuyler, Kenward Elmslie, Frank Lima,
Bill Berkson, Joe Ceravolo, Ted Berrigan,
Allan Kaplan, Ron Padgett, Dick Gallup,
Peter Schjeldahl, Joe Brainard, John Giorno, Anne Waldman,
Michael Brownstein, Lewis Warsh, David Shapiro and I,
chartered a bus,
and went to visit the Hart Crane monument in Cleveland.

We returned on April 24th, refreshed, amused and ready to write.
The budding plants and flowers, after their endless
absence during the harsh winter, gave us all
the feeling of being in love for the first time.
That is, after the harsh winter
of white snow and cold wandering visions,
as the windows rattled in the wind, when the floors
creaked in the midst of our pondering memories and complaints,
and when from the pitch of a snowy night the furious wolf,
dripping blood from the gaping jar of his mouth,
pacing the shelves in flames,
reminded us of the terrible days of Hart Crane,
when people were not as kind to poets as they are today.

In the beginning nothing is congenial, not even the world
not even your notes. In the middle many things are pleasant
and even towards the end, but the end is self-explanatory,
and full of asides and commas with people to clean up the room.
Then you feel that Handel is truly your friend.
His singers send you to glory,
as his music is a preservative, for him not you.

FOR IRMA

A peaceful bite of hamburger and your mind is blown into space,
going on for some time while the long roots of space
dig into your language and the fuel pitches its tents and talks to you.

You escape from this passively and pay the check. Your mind
is occupied, backing across the Brooklyn Bridge,
the serenity of the city to blind you with the sun,
and going through you into Brooklyn Heights.
It is April as you keep from bursting. In Córdoba and Seville
the churches enclose you and you think what you wish.
On Fifth Avenue you combine the words and cross the street,
between or among the starry buildings.
If the moon rises you will see the city.

You exhale and ideas fall from your mouth. The vowels are raised
and become diphthongs and soon you are speaking Modern English,
fighting the Germans, pressured into study and learning,
crowding into the forest of tables to eat.

1

The lion roars his possibilities over the phone,
and is himself the possibility that one does not
see things clearly after months of the sun and the moon
alternating the horizon with euphemisms,
the silver cup of the past, clattering,
the paper cup of the present,
the elegant plastic goblet of the future
in the far crummy distance of magazines
waiting for weeks and crowds to run off at the mouth;
headaches in the afternoon,
the darkened museum of streets at evening,
a quick bounce into the brief country air for recovery,
where American as I am I send up my words to the presidents:

> "O sexual drunkenness of the twenties,
> Corny proletarianism of the thirties,
> Carmen Miranda movies of the forties,
> Adolescent sadism of the fifties,
> Mindless pacifism of the sixties, the Negroes
> losing their humor and forming their Mafia,
> the comic improvements of the seventies on television,
> the turn of the century and beyond,
> when archaic English will be gleaned from our lives
> where they float in the carbonized air."

The presidents ignore my vocatives. They saw
that I was not obstreperous enough to write,

when the first for whom I voted was shot through the neck
on television and by word of mouth.

But I have an answer for everything.

And news comes to life; I see it and hear it. The fires
rage or don't rage and doubt
burns in any event. You read poetry or don't read it
pleased with your sensitivity in any event,
finding energy for your life in some way as the air waits for the dawn
on 1st September to give it breath for a month
and again for October. After 40 one becomes a lecher,
period; but how can you doubt that we will meet and love forever
on a great enormity of clouds?

2

The bacon too carries on its modest love affair.
When it is tired of eggs, we insert hors d'oeuvres, muffins,
waffles and sandwiches. The bacon too sits by the sea
in its coating of ancient sand. The bacon, it must be admitted,
is washed soon away legless with the tide, and the sun goes down
in the country life not knowing what is to be produced.
And you, on vacation in nervous retirement in the nineties,
some of you admirable and some despicable,
decades of adequate jobs and salaries, an apartment
or house and someone to live with you,
children to keep you aware of the time,
the years of essays and scriptwriting,

you speak at last from massy age to a sea of admiring faces,
one of which gleams with an absolute adoration
and falls over the railing.
That's all I can say now about the nineties
except godspeed to its comeback in the twenties.

I am still in the sixties however, the ivory gulls,
the gliding farmland, carrion, garbage and eggs,
marine invertebrates,
animals priding themselves on their lives, as they climb the trees
and eat the leaves, live in cool springs or under logs and stones,
or in comfortable damp cavities in the earth.
There are many animals as I walk in the silver night
to whom I am reminiscent of something else.
Which occurs as the sea rolls over the weeds,
on the coastal provinces each with its huddled poor and peculiar thoughts,
each thought a quest for searching minds.
We go back to our sautéed rainbow trout, or another dish;
we go back to our account books and taxes;
you will be ruined by 36, he says;
the steak falls to the floor;
the fish it came from howls in the midnight void.
As far as going to bed with everyone goes
you climb some stairs and end at the curve of your skull;
as far as your American epic and talking to the presidents goes
you went to the end and got off;
the sixties are long uncorked and you are only
the basis for this eight o'clock and the good and the bad.

The muse's perfume drifts across the keys;
she is in the room promising a caress,
a draft alive within my ear,
an air of coolness and drowsy inertia.

A sprite, a messenger of the muse,
flies above the swelling earth,
her watery swarms of intoxication
in showers of bees on our scattered parts,
strewn in a system of earliest simplicity.

In the blank moments of the day and night
the blood of divinity rushes our senses,
surrounding our breathless repose
on land come up from the sea to dry
with nothing familiar begun to exist.

Old in our dream familiar things spring up.
A truck rolls forward stringing wire,
the dizzy feel of the empty sky,
a woman naked and arched,
falling so that I enter without limit.

Here are the wheels of the new kingdom and here,
here are the radical tires. You believe me of course, a plant,
a cup, who have demonstrated affectionate indifference,
the blundering forest charm plunked you into, number 32.
We end thoughtfully, with three dots,
in contrast to the inertness of the ball.

In the discussion above I spoke of the inertness of the ball.
The numbers get higher, in sequence. A sequence
is a godsend, another cloud in the Alps and the air.

FOR JASPER JOHNS

The vaporous evils of drink maneuver your steps,
through the channels of sociability.
You wait for ideas,
they expand the significance of your birth
from the oblivion of earlier ages,
when the world collapsed in an infernal hurricane
or some highly nervous state.

With their persistence the ruddy charm of English reserve
turns to glowing Irish bullshit,
and your answers to questions recede
as in deep philosophical sleep.
Your friends adjust to malice and deceit,
and to the sheer pleasure of giving a sharp answer.
No one is safe from malice and deceit
or from the pleasure of giving a sharp answer,
even the solitary shepherd, in his lonely pastoral beauty,
will give one to his sheep.

Everyone sleeps, but awake and there are difficulties,
as in sleep there are numerous voices.
Get up. Disturb not her magic sleep

in which you remain in voluptuous pursuit,
intoxicated, and billowing clouds of messengers
sent to the end of the somnolent world with your message
which comes with the evils of drink to the walls of the morning;

where you abandon your frivolous actions and vain desires,
the unpleasantness, distractions and disappointing follies,
the worries, reverses, slander and gossip,
the crowds of threatening enemies,
as intrigues are woven about you
as about any unlucky person;

and where spring stirs in cloudless flight
over the surface where the birds stop
short of my efforts beneath. A halo appears through the clouds
and today will be a successful day, the magnificent sun
driving my greatest abilities forth, its burgeoning light
dissolving idleness and despair,
to incite the highest invention, prosperity
and contentment, not dissipation and foolishness
but the opposite, overwhelming achievement and love.

The sky is cut into sections and put on a frame.
Part of the sky is covered with clouds.
Machines rise and descend.
The portions of the sky blend together.
The plot requires a flowing river.
It comes down from the mountains.
A road winds parallel to the river.
Fish are set in motion.
The people in the shops and on the streets move.
The clouds go from one end of the sky to the other.
The arms and the hands are loose and relaxed.
Conversation comes spontaneously.
It is a few years later.
The next four years show great achievement.
The remaining years are disappointing.

The lead drains from your heart on the left side,
and further down, on Third Avenue, people
seem to trail after you, on a sort of patrol
across from the cavernous idea of Queens,
my demand for it having created the supply;
like a beautiful four room apartment for a hundred dollars
and furnished like a longing for the forties,
a rich lemon or lime in a drink away from here,
the America of the sixties harnessing our potentials.

The torch flies around our heads,
the manifesto sinks to the ground
from which it springs every spring
as its metaphor is a metaphor of activity;
hanging before the shimmering soil
where we work as on a stupid shoulder of veal
combined with it in a spurious oath of friendship
and leaving it as a party to a duel.

You sleep with the potato of metaphor in your stomach,
the novelty of an imminent American Baroque and the hair
resting on your arm in the full chill of a distant corps de ballet,
and are happy page after page in glorious speculation
in whichever century speaks to you.

The Allegorical Figure of Brooklyn is right here,
there where you're standing, and here's how it works.
The lamps go on and we walk through miles of parks;
the rain and the sleet are brought on, we travel
to Queens for two weeks of vacation; the sun returns
and the grass and farms, the villages of Brooklyn
continue to grow, and the spacious terrace and
oily sand of Brooklyn breathe, and are rocked slowly
by the Figure, and back toward home on the BMT
we smile at the tender Figure and wave goodbye.

Poem

FOR FRANK LIMA

In beautiful English, in the same breath on the same day
(English without a pure vowel to its name, even my voices,
which are never wrong, slur their vowels to oblivion)
we absorb the grueling climate of modern life,
the anarchistic wings and rancid depths
of its massive societal implications.

So we keep moving, from surrealistic symbolism
to the dramatic allegory of symbolistic realism,
or somewhere else, in constellations of luminosity,
on the way to true metaphorical existence,
resembling not twins nor archers nor crabs
but a vivid provocative tentativeness, golden phlox
to illumine the clammy humors of the body,
and with cool imperturbable emotionalism
invaginating the passive oaf of narration.

Though if we get flop-sweat now, writing in our youth,
how will our nerves react when the laureateship
is delivered to us doddering, bloated with abstractions
propped by Parnassian phlegm, into our rheumy hands.
Why don't we admit it, the wreath
would stupify the citric edges of our spleen,
our possible fame at any rate booted asunder by the Novel,
in the fatiguing quest for its ultimate poetic title,
and at present among the elements we look for a sort of passage,
in the wake of Science the heads they have called and won
but are not sublime as the tails with which we will lose
which have not yet killed us and are not tails or news.

Even in bountiful spring, when golf
emerges from its cool place for the rich and fanatic,
the late afternoon brings the weight of the world,
and the pound of digesting lunch
wages hectic battle with my stomach and its forces
who achieve their daily phyrric success.
It is not surprising that one gets into one's poem
for these difficult hours, and floats off,
the water sublime with motionless adjectives
and steering with the gentle miniature verbs
who with calm indifference move the poem
to the conclusion of the opposite shore,
to debark in the silence of gastric distress.

But to begin, pushed off with a phrase
and the romantic adieux of the nightingales
flown in from a century of strangulation
to hover above your gliding prow
as it cuts the shimmering paper
as you figure your taxes in this listless hour
in a nearby furrow of the brain
where it is hard to stick to the point of all this,
and you find that the government will owe you money
and the poem drains away
from the things that are your own
and from which your visitors digress.

St. John goes to the field, in blue and gray,
the colors of the American Civil War.
God remains above, in blood red and gold; blood red
to remind us of our mortality.
Air comes through the grate in a steady flow.
Christ is triumphant.
People surround Christ Triumphant.
I have made their faces beet red.
I am the salt air and the dazzling sunshine.

At long last, as the search for impressions continues,
a letter from a company, in this capacious month,
with a remonstrance that really moves me,
and with scalding exactitude, like being calm
before your only and tremendous possibility.

It is the inner chamber of the year, June,
the risen buildings filled with a summer transparency,
open doors and sliding windows
and tubes for the warm and cool life-giving air
to support the activity within.
In these surroundings one grows dignified and luxurious,
neither young by the standards of America
nor middle-aged by the standards of middle age.
One hurries about, each with a simple expression of tragedy,
each with a different style and theme.

In the buildings 1967 has been the year of the pervert,
silly instead of eloquent, amused instead of elated,
and since you like dot dot dot, fill in the blank,
you're as much of a pervert as anyone,
waiting for the Greenport train,
waiting for the Montauk train,
you permit only what goes with your life,
and understand the summer by wearing a tie in August.
You ignore it by crossing Houston Street with everyone else,
comparing it to the coming of autumn.
You feel horny instead of longing,
and irritable instead of melancholy.
There are times when the rumbling subway
zeroes in for a serious conclusion,
and times when 16th century dandyism of language dropping from the sky
is the most important thing, my little pancake,
though real birds fly in the cold air and people walk in it.

Today is Thursday, the twentieth day of September, 1967.
It is the two hundred and sixty-third day of the year,
with a hundred and two days left to go.

Yes but what's your point?

The point is my play is being done considerable damage.
I am forced to speak to the characters (moving stage center)
who emit farts and impossible conjectures.
If they walk things happen to their feet;
if they think then it's their heads.
The blood rushes here and there as ink,
but indiscriminate and colorless.

I had wanted yellow ink, to show the difficulties
of being Jewish; white ink, for the troublesomeness of purity;
and purple, the problems faced by novelists.

But the characters will irritate and amuse themselves
in a sodden jungle of policy
and leave me with the tundra of the script.

In the Time/Life Building,
companion to architectural regret,
a feeling wells up among the thirty years which fate
in a casual gesture
has bestowed on my person.
A crowd collects as I have fainted with astonishment
from the abundance fate has collected in its Western Heaven,
and inflated higher than even the stones
the seat of the air. From my affliction, through the crowd,
on the seat of the air, I see a little nip in the air
this September, which begins a walk in the park.

(FOR BOB, DIANE, HENRY, IRMA AND MYSELF)

Very clever, starting this poem now,
with an aerial view of Cleveland and a contemplation of industry,
chevrons, workers in Brooklyn alive in their socialist realism,
atomies, or tiny beings, on the way to an assignation with Asclepius,
having given us gradual glottal closure, in short making us sick—
All this because Irma was giving Bob, Diane and Henry all the margaritas
and even my imminent entrance spiced with witty obscenities
could not compensate for that endless present of their lack.
How uninteresting! to write as an assuasive interlude in retrospect,
a guest to slowly undermine my hospitality and cheer
and who is not grateful; as one is or should be for the prophecies
(Blake was right Whitman was wrong) of the heated past,
and for those who pit the olives for you
and for the lithograph emerging from the press
as every lithograph from 1798 on, rustles a little, in salute.
What a strange salute. I look at the Himalayas;
they neither sit nor stand, neither dead nor alive but are,
so one is informed, inert, the way one feels
after a publication waiting for the next one,
after a reading waiting for Aphrodite.
But our minds wander, don't they,
and we have made grievous mistakes
and even if they're not grievous our minds get soggy
from the classical exercise of the person or persons of our choice,
which being the grand entree to the problems of life
and the litter made beautiful by history . . .
But your headache is gone!

GARCILASO DE LA VEGA

The roads are in poor condition,
and there is no energy to move on them.
When one leaves
there are only the same things.

Death watches,
while I observe my life,
fate, and the inescapable list
of unfortunate things I have done.

In this brief time
I seem not to resist my inclinations
and the certainty of death
confuses their remedy.

LUIS DE GÓNGORA

Meanwhile, to compete with your hair, the sun
in flowering gold burns in vain;
your sumptuous forehead ignores
the whiteness of a beautiful sea of wavering lilies.

More eyes watch the parting of your lips,
and close with unbearable passion,
than are moved by the reaching flowers of earliest spring,
and your flawless neck is more than delicate crystal.

Enjoy your neck, lips, hair and radiant face
until what you will see as your golden age,
in its gold, fields of flowers and comparisons to crystal

reaches not only lead and the scattered crumbs of dead violets
but all of us together
come to the earth, dust, smoke and their shadow of nothing.

GUSTAVO ADOLFO BÉCQUER

Giant waves will fall on some remote shore,
and carry me there wrapped in their foam.

A hurricane tears the leaves from a forest,
and brings me with its whirlwind across the sky.

Lightning has frozen the clouds in my fear,
blinding its dark impulse.

The dizziness of these places, in my memory,
is with me in my grief.

Custard voices and sunrise on the platform, events
which interesting or not replace some others.
One can see that you have had no practice
and that you wait for a train until the sky is orange
and the platform is mush.

We are taller on the average than our ancestors,
and so our buildings are also taller,
with a lack, morning and evening March and September,
of seriousness, that amuses this endless
re-issue of yourself, on the train wondering
why your ancestors ever left England
where they could sit and be English in the course of events
without the embarrassment of subject matter.

But after all one comes to a sane decision in the summer stillness,
sex, the great universal pleasure, getting up and lying down,
caught on to at once.

1

It begins to get dark, the foggy air gets chilly.
We take the jar and descend from the hills.
Here are some pebbles. We put them in the jar.
We find a necktie, and put it around the jar.
The jar is wearing a tie. The jar speaks:

  "I remember the turnips in the fields.
    I remember the creatures eating and eating."

A rooster crows. Flies buzz. The jar
will receive its reward.

2

The years go by. Many people are saved
and many fall into the ravine.
Some people are handsome and some
are as ugly as trolls. Robert sighs:

  "There is no reason for me to work. They
    lead me through the gate and up the sidewalk.
    In my basement home I go to the darkest corner, the
    red woollen blanket around me, repose my hands and sleep."

Here we all are, painting, poetry and music,
having a soda at our favorite fountain,
talking away and bloated with triumph:
For with bouquets and calling for another drink
we have won, the unfortunate century
redeemed by our sensibilities.

But remember that you are writing poetry,
and when the past wells up with its veil
it is only a line running before another,
and the draft from approaching January
a device to fill you with winter,
as the streets when someone dies are pages
and the television brings you to a quiet world.

Turbulent specks swimming for six informative years,
chops and lines in the stomach and dreams,
rosé waterfall splashing the lines and the floor
the fog of the five boroughs you waited for,
a November Wordsworth glaze of starry Vermont,
under the protective wings of arcs of fiery leaves;
also disgusted, and numbed by the smoke of contestants,
pressed by attacks on germs and dust,
or throbbing pains in the blood.

But perhaps you liked some of it very much,
comparing it here in transient bloom
to a childish stumbling Paradise Lost,
short not only of cashable greenbacks,
but the wind denying the lungs
of spiritual things as well, gasping ethereal frogs,
chips of ancient tile and civilized pottery,
which make shopping and spending more enjoyable.

One cannot know what I mean and sincerity
has entered as fashion biting its nails
and tribal rhetoric waits in the wings.
Cruel time waits further on with ridiculous simplicity,
and what melancholy ship you chose
at the fork of the earth,
whether it is you meaning myself
or the you of a timeless thought,
carries you unimportant and forgetful in the water.

Coleridge has told you how poignantly he felt,
and so have I.
I have never known anyone, not for a second,
a finger going from the rest,
an arm thread by thread in the same way,
the vanishing trip which makes up my life.